RYAN EARLEY

TABLE OF CONTENTS

A Pelican Book

Teaching Tips for Caregivers and Teachers:

Research shows that one of the best ways for students to learn a new topic is to read about it.

Before Reading

- Read the title and predict what the book will be about.
- Read the "Words to Know" and discuss the meaning of each word.
- Read the back cover to see what the book is about.

During Reading

- When a student gets to a word that is unknown, ask them to look at the rest of the sentence to find clues to help with the meaning of the unknown word.
- Motivate students with praise and encouragement.

After Reading

- Discuss the main idea of the book.
- Ask students to give one detail that they learned in the book.

Sight Words

a	help	some
all	is	take
have	most	this

Words to Know

garbage truck

hopper

lift

trash

wheels

This is a
garbage truck.

garbage truck

All garbage trucks have **wheels**.

NOTICE
DANGER
DANGER
wheel

Some garbage trucks have a **lift**.

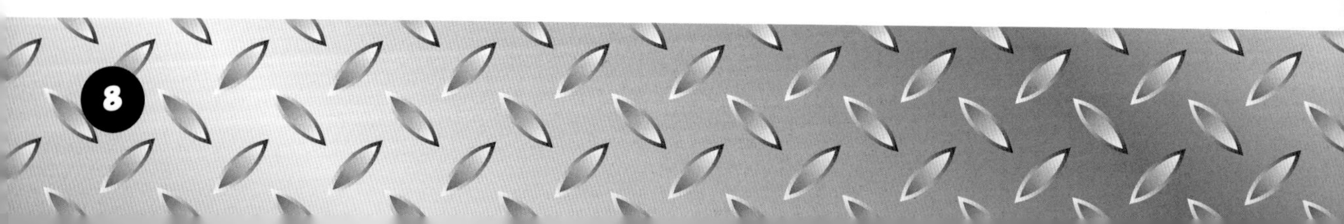

lift

Most garbage trucks have a **hopper**.

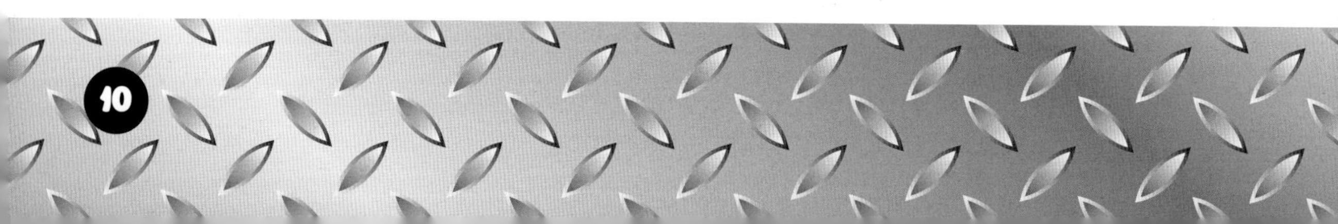

hopper

All garbage trucks take **trash**.

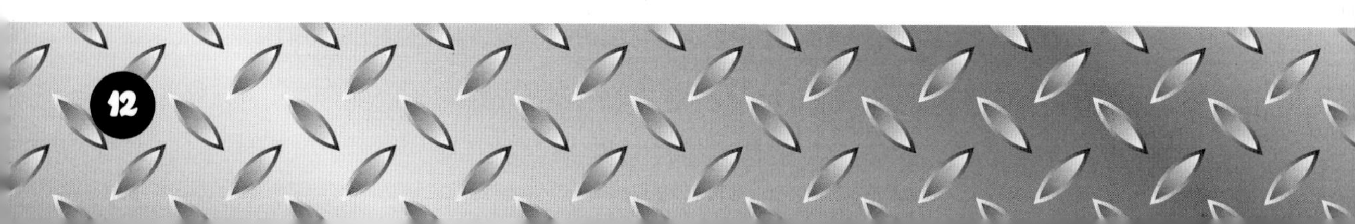

trash